Gods Sovereignty Within
The Number Two

By Tim Patton

Draft2Digital.com

FOREWORD

All numbers have a spiritual meaning attached to them. The spiritual implication of the use of the number Two in the Bible illustrates Gods sovereignty and symbolizes the divine counsel of God. Scriptural symbolism has meaning and relevance thus it must be interpreted by using scripture. The arithmography of scripture is the doctrine of the word established by numbers and the precision in which they fall into place. Such is the study of Bible numbers and their application to the truth. We will look for the message revealed in each of these set of Twos as God opens our understanding and blesses us with the deeper truths of His Word. These numerical phenomena thus prove the inspiration of the scriptures comes from the one who is, who was, and is to come. Prophecies frequently shroud their true meaning within numbers woven throughout the pages of the Bible. The repetition of prophetic events through types and shadows is just another way God demonstrates his sovereignty. The significance of the word corresponds with the significance of the number of times it occurs. In one, we have the promise and prediction and the other, the performance and the fulfillment. First the type or the shadow then the reality and substance. This remarkable relationship between them proves its divine design and establishes the spiritual significance of the number. Sometime typologies are hidden in mysteries that lay dormant until the revelation is given, such as Genesis 2:23 "For this reason a man shall leave his father and mother and be joined to his wife and the Two shall become one flesh." No scripture is to be interpreted without regard to the relation in which it stands to the other parts. Not only does one scripture support and illuminate another but very often one passage supplements and augments another. This is written to all who will believe with the purpose of leading men to Christ, because everything in the gospel illustrates and demonstrates his providence.

TABLE OF CONTENTS

Gods Sovereignty within the Number Two

- Two Days
- Two Stages
- Two Wives
- Two Raptures
- Two End Time Signs
- Two Mysteries
- Two Tribulations
- Two Churches
- Two Witnesses
- Two Spirits
- Two Kingdoms
- Two Names
- Two-Edged Sword

INTRODUCTION

In the beginning, there were Two lights and Two trees, Two seeds and Two brothers, Two bloodlines, and Two judgments. Two birds were sent out from Noah's ark, and Two angels were sent to Sodom. Pharaoh and Joseph both had Two dreams, and there were Two magicians. There were Two tablets of the testimony, Two goats, Two stones, Two trumpets, Two pillars, Two cherubims, and Two spies. There are Two olive trees and Two anointed ones, Two false witnesses, and Two criminals. Two end time signs and Two praiseworthy churches. Two have been raptured and there are Two days of the Lord.

From this quick synopsis, we are able to discern something rather unique when it comes to the number Two. As we delve further into each occurrence, we will unravel the truth behind it. It's our duty as well as privilege to diligently examine God's Word. The number Two found in scripture is a mystery hidden in typology and symbols used to describe God's divine plan being revealed through revelation. The first mention in scripture of anything invariably defines its meaning and forecasts its subsequent significance. We see first the shadow and then the substance or type.

Prophecy, either in direct utterance or in symbolic type, is the divine autograph upon the sacred page, the authority and the absolute sufficiency of God. Prophecy is the manifestation of the word of God and corresponds with the work of Christ and its significance within the numbers themselves.

"And for that dream was doubled unto Pharaoh twice, it is because the thing is established by God and God will shortly bring it to pass." Genesis 41:32

PREFACE

The revelation of God throughout the Bible is perfect, complete, and progressive in its unveiling. The sovereignty of God is absolute and infinite. It's our privilege and obligation to search out these scriptures prayerfully and carefully, looking to the Holy Spirit for guidance, to understand what God is giving us by his spirit. It's important to pray for the interpretation, and the Lord will be faithful in giving us this understanding. For he is the Alpha and Omega, proclaiming he was at the beginning of creation and at the end.

Sometimes we find a narrative in which there are many intended parallelisms and must discern between the figurative and the literal interpretation. A key to this is the use of first mention as well as subsequent occurrences. Prophetic scripture may also refer to Two events separated by a significant time period. By analyzing the fulfillment of Bible prophecy using the principles of recognition and realization, it can be demonstrated that God reveals, unveils, and uncovers those things by his spirit. We will soon discover that certain passages have distinctions between prophecy and mystery, providing the time is ripe for unfolding God's secret purpose.

Such comparative study will give us much light, and the ability to see what we have never seen before. The twofold meaning is such that it may mean merely what is kept hidden or it may mean something understood only by the initiated or maybe both at the same time. To discover the principle recording fulfillment of prophecy we have Two basic principles. One is to interpret prophecy according to its spiritual meaning and hence it has a reference to an implied fulfillment, the other according to the letter thus referring to a literal fulfillment. The fulfillment of any single prophecy is but the sovereignty of God in operation. It's the demonstration of what he has declared. God foreordains everything which comes to pass, as he is working out his eternal purpose. A type is an event, person or institution that foreshadows something that will come, but is not revealed until after the fact, basically an unspoken prophecy. Any fulfillment of Bible prophecy demonstrates the validity of the power, presence and providence of the almighty. The sovereignty of God, which means he is in control of the universe and all things. He rules over all superintending humanity without violating mans ability to choose.

A Dual-purpose prophecy - After a prophecy is given and fulfilled, it's also typological of a future prophecy yet to be fulfilled. The number Two is maintained throughout Scripture 1,065 times and will help show us the spiritual significance of this. One of its meanings is <u>union</u>. It came to stand for strengthening, courage, and confirmation. Two were far stronger and more effective than one. Redoubled energy uniting into one powerful force, such as Christ and the church. To bear true witness to the Lord we must be in union with Christ and separated from the world.

"For Two shall become one flesh."
Genesis 2:24

"Two are better than one because they have a good reward for their labor." Ecclesiastes 3:9

"Where Two are gathered together in my name there I am in the midst of them."
Matthew 18:24

"If Two of you shall agree on Earth as touching anything that they shall ask, it shall be done for them of my Father who is in heaven."
Matthew 18:19

Two is also the number of <u>Witness.</u>

"It is also written in your law that the testimony of Two men is true." John 8:17

"Out of the mouth of Two witnesses every word shall be established." Matthew 8:16

There was a symbolic significance in the fact that Jesus sent his disciples forth Two by Two. Angels usually came as a witness in Twos as with Abraham, the sepulcher and the ascension. John sent Two disciples to ask if Jesus was the Christ, and the Two sons of thunder asked if they could sit on either side of Christ in heaven.

Lastly, the number Two is associated with <u>division</u>.

"Suppose ye that I am come to bring peace on the earth? I tell you nay. But rather <u>division</u>, for from henceforth there shall be five in one house divided, three against Two and Two against three." Luke 12:51

"No man can serve Two masters, for either he will hate the one and love the other, or else he will hold to one and despise the other." Matthew 6:4

Since Two is the first divisible number in the Bible, it expresses Two thoughts for us to consider. Two men went up to the temple to pray, one was justified and the other exalted himself. The Two men crucified next to Jesus had different options; one accepted and received Jesus, the other did not. Jesus said "but be shod with sandals and not put on Two coats" or don't be double minded.

Likewise, there are Two opposing spirits in the world, the spirit of truth and the spirit of error. We will examine all these points for all scripture is profitable. These striking sets of Two encapsulates God's panoramic plans for humanity. The numbers interwoven within the Bible establish their inspiration as they fall into their place to unfold God's pattern throughout the ages. Notice how frequently the same number is used. These verses seem to be specially marked in this way to draw our attention to them and bring out an important truth. The first use of a number invariably gives a clue to its spiritual meaning. The infinite mind of God devised this system of numbers and inspired men to record them in his word. God is always intentional, and the number Two is an integrity provided, showing us that God has indeed established it. The Holy Spirit uses this hidden arithmetic to prove the truth of God's word. Prophets frequently have a double meaning and refer to different events, one near and the other remote. One temporal and the other eternal. What has not been fulfilled in the first must apply to the second. What has already been fulfilled may be considered as typical of what remains to be accomplished. It's the purpose of God to give the near and the far view so that the fulfillment of the first should be the assurance of the fulfillment of the other.

The Lord always gives a foretaste of the outline of a deeper life before he leads us into the full experience of it. God's sovereignty reigns supreme and is displayed all throughout the Bible, especially witnessed by the number Two. Patterns begin to emerge as we see these uncanny sets of Two unfold. Prophecy is but the manifestation of God's eternal presence foretold in innumerable instances. God is sovereign and his will is supreme which guarantees the fulfillment of prophecy. May we reverently search the more sure word of prophecy with gratitude for those things which God has pleased to unveil and the things which much must shortly come to pass.

TWO LIGHTS

"I am the light of the world, he who follows me shall not walk in darkness but have the light of life." John 8:12

First Light

At creation, natural light was the first thing produced by God. At the new creation, spiritual light is the first thing given to illuminate the truth.

"In thy light shall we see light." Psalms 36:9

We follow that light which alone illuminates the darkness to lift our eyes to the Word who is the life and light of everything. God said let there be light and so light was produced by the Word, the acting of the Holy Spirit. This light is also the light of salvation bringing us back to God the Father. When the spirit of God casts light upon the scriptures the teachings are made clear.

"The entrance of thy words giveth light" Psalms 119.

By grace, we come to God as he also comes to us in grace. God has revealed himself in this light of his grace through the gospel.

Light is in the word of God but the lamp is in us. Once his word shines on us, it's saving grace, once we see its mercy. We in Christ are a light to the world, so let us be sons of light. The church glorifies God by radiating his light in the world.

"In him was life and the life was the light of men." John 1:4

"Come let us walk in the light of the Lord." Isaiah 2:5

"The Lord is my light and my salvation." Psalms 27:1

By nature, fallen man is in a state of darkness with respect to God. Not until he is renewed in the spirit of his mind by the Holy Spirit can he see things in God's light. The darkness of the world will once again be shattered and displaced by the Lord Jesus, the one true light at his second coming.

Second Light

"For God who commanded the light to shine on the darkness has shined into our hearts, to give light of the knowledge of the glory of God in the face of Jesus Christ." 2 Corinthians 4:6

Spiritual Birth is only possible by receiving him who is the light, through believing in him we are brought into the unity of faith. This unity of faith is the light of fellowship, and walking in the light displays our faith and fellowship.

"Let your light so shine before men that they may see your good works and glorify your Father which is in heaven." Matthew 5:16

The first light is the light that belongs to God but is shed upon us, the second is the knowledge imparted by that light. Only when there is light coming from God may we see, for God is light.

TWO TREES

The Forbidden Tree

"Of every tree of the garden thou mayest freely eat but of the tree of the knowledge of good and evil thou shall not eat of it, for in the day that thou eatest thereof thou shall surely die."
Genesis 2:17

The Two trees represent Two plans of life, the divine and the human. The purpose of the Two trees was the exercise of free choice. The tree of life is God himself, for God is life, the source and goal of life. The fruit is Jesus Christ or God in a receivable form. The other tree produces self sufficiency and acting apart from God. Independent living from the soul usurping the place of the spirit.

This forbidden tree was pleasant to look at ("The lust of the eyes") which also corresponded to the offer of the Lord's temptation to all the kingdoms of the world. It was good to eat ("The lust of the flesh") which corresponded to the Lord's temptation to turn the stones into bread. It was said to make one wise, ("The pride of life") which corresponded to the Lord's temptation to throw himself from the pinnacle of the temple.

This tree took away our spiritual connection to God and God didn't want spiritually dead people to live forever so he barred them from the second tree, the Tree of Life. For to be immortal and continue in this fallen same condition would surely be the second death. Adam's sin was nothing less than acting outside of God according to his own will. Thus in Adam we all become sinners, subject to the law and deserving of God's wrath, because what is in us by nature is subject to the law of sin and death. When we receive the son of God, we not only receive the forgiveness of sins, but we receive life both now and eternally. Man's actions should not be governed by the knowledge of good and evil but should be motivated by the sense of obedience and find our right and wrong in God. Faith is the principle by which we obtain life, so obedience is the principle by which that life is lived out. Apart from his own power, God is not interested in any other. Apart from his own will, God is not satisfied with anything else. We must rely on his will and depend on his grace.

The Tree of Life

"I am the way, the truth, and the life." John 14:6

Jesus came in the likeness of sinful flesh and poured out his soul unto death on this tree to bring us back into fellowship with our Father. This sets us free and releases the life of Christ in us which is the antidote to the death in Adam. This new creation is enthroned with the authority of Christ. There is a design antithesis in the fact by eating of the forbidden tree, man lost his spiritual life and so by eating of the tree of life man obtains spiritual and eternal life. Eating is the symbol of communion and fellowship with God. The tree of life is a symbol of Christ himself giving immortality.

TWO ADAMS

First Adam

"The first man Adam was made a living soul, the last Adam was made a quickening spirit."
1 Corinthians 15:47

Adam was created with a mind to know God, a heart to love God, and a will to obey God. Adam was free in that he could choose to obey God by submitting his will with the will of God. Adam was deceived in the mind first, then the heart to doubt. This doubt produced rebellion which manifested as lawlessness. Adam was overruled by his emotion which resulted in independence, and so Adam rebelled when he declared his independence from God. His spirit fell under the influence of his soul and sin rendered the soul independent. This flesh became man's nature and developed abnormal cravings which enticed the soul. Adam, in his independence and submission to his wife instead of God, was deceived and the devil usurped his authority. The forbidden tree produced this nature of rebellion, proud and selfish. Adam's nature was changed from untried innocence to transgression and since the root was corrupted, so too his seed bore corruption.

Last Adam

"For as in Adam all die, even so in Christ shall all be made alive." 1 Corinthians 15:22

In Eden there was a double subversion of the delegated and direct authority of God. There was a rebellion as well as sin and in so sin entered the world. The first Adam was assigned the role of a servant to dress the garden and forsook it to aspire to become like God. The last Adam was God who took on the role of a servant to set us free. There is only one who is worthy of the deed of the domain and to rule over Earth. Jesus is the rightful ruler of Adam's domain because he redeems and restores Adam's offspring back to the Father. Christ in laying down his life for us vindicated the majesty and truth of God which Adam had so grievously dishonored aspiring to be equal with God.

Reversing the fall exhibits the riches of grace, mercy, and wisdom of the Most High because where sin abounded, grace did much more abound. Adam received unmerited favor and a promise of saving grace through the seed that was to come. As with the first Adam, we all inherited his nature and so it is also with the last Adam. As we are in Christ, everything that belongs to him belongs to us, we have inherited patience, holiness and humility. As long as we stay in him, we possess these virtues. The hidden prophetic meaning behind this number is most important emphasizing the beginning of the seed plot with Two seed lines.

TWO SEEDS

"And I will put enmity between thee and the woman and between thy seed and her seed. It shall bruise thy head, and thou shall bruise his heel." Genesis 3:15

Seed of the Serpent

As a result of the fall, a war of Two seeds began. Satan's course of action was to contaminate the people through whom the promise of the Messiah, savior, and redeemer of the world would come. Beginning in Genesis, the watchers polluted the DNA to genetically manipulate the bloodline. Satan implemented his plan to corrupt the seed that would one day crush his head. His strategy of physical and spiritual contamination passed through Adam's seed to prevent the kingsman redeemer from coming to fruition. The children of Israel being the appointed channel through which the Messiah was to come, became the object of continued enmity and assaults such as famines, Pharaoh's edict to destroy all male children, the assaults of the Canaanites, the plot of Haman and more.

Seed of the Woman

"For this purpose, the son of God appeared to destroy the works of the devil." 1 John 3:8

God of course had prearranged and designed a plan of restoration and salvation even before he created the world. Through the seed of the woman, Jesus would destroy Satan and redeem humanity. True humanity needed to be preserved so that a human savior could be brought to this world to save mankind. Genetically connected to the seed of Abraham and the bloodline of David, Jesus would fulfill prophecy crushing the head of the serpent and bringing salvation. To avoid sharing in the tainted blood of Adam, Jesus would come from a virgin via the Holy Ghost.

"Behold a virgin shall conceive and bear a son and shall call his name Immanuel." Isaiah 7:14

This promise shows the divine method of the redeemers' conception and birth. Christ came to destroy the works of the devil. For that purpose was he born, for that purpose did he live, and for that purpose did he die.

Putting enmity between the Two seeds was the commencement of God's plan of mercy and the first act of grace. This conflict still exists in his seed today, we who are in Christ are at enmity being treated with contempt and anger, which is proof of the enmity. The forces of darkness continue to buffet Christ's body trying to destroy the seed of God's chosen. Yet the battle is the Lord's, and the victory falls to him. From the beginning, Satan schemed through Cain to kill his brother from whom the promise seed would come. In Jesus first coming, we see the bruising of the heel with him laying down his life. With his second coming, we will see the crushing of the serpent's head when he is cast into the abyss.

TWO BROTHERS

Let's mark the spiritual truth that lies behind this number used here, for there was <u>division</u> between the Two brothers. Abel presented his sacrifice to God in faith. He acknowledged he was a sinner, and in offering a lamb as a substitute, he saw it satisfying God's divine judgment, and by faith that God would accept him. A blood sacrifice is necessary to take away sin, an innocent life dying to symbolically cover sin and restore fellowship with God. This ritual was God's prescribed pattern until the ultimate sacrifice was made on the cross. Abel typifies the spiritual man who realizes their hope lies outside of themselves in another and casts themselves upon God's grace.

Cain denied that he was a fallen creature, denied he was a guilty sinner with a sin nature and deliberately ignored God's demand for a sacrificial substitute. He insisted on approaching God on the ground of personal worthiness. He offered the fruits of the ground which God had cursed, the work of his own hands. So, Cain represents the natural man offering fruit in the form of moral character, unselfish deeds, and charitable works. One is faith, the other works; one is grace, the other human merit; one is life, the other death.

As a result of the contamination from the fallen angels, sin spread forth and reigned on earth. God would have no other choice but to send judgement. There's always a prophetic warning first, then God removes his people, and judgment falls. God in his infinite mercy provides an ark of safety for all who will listen to his voice from the coming judgment on this world, and through faith in him, who is the resurrection and the life.

TWO GREAT JUDGEMENTS

The Flood

"For God did not spare the ancient world but saved Noah, one of eight people a preacher of righteousness, bringing in the flood on the world of the ungodly." 2 Peter 2:5

Noah's generation was filled with violence, corruption, murder, abortion, deceit, adultery, rebellion, and independence. The whole Earth was corrupted by the works of the watchers through genetic engineering and mixing species. Except for Noah who trusted God and was a preacher of righteousness, being a man of faith and genetically pure, he built the ark.

"And of every living thing of all flesh, Two of every sort shalt thou bring into the ark." Genesis 6:18

Noah's faith laid hold of things not seen as yet. He was an heir of righteousness which is by faith, and a witness against the ungodly.

The Fire

"Because the outcry against Sodom and Gomorrah is great, and because their sin is very grave." Genesis 18:20

What we see is a pattern throughout history of people defying God even in the face of judgment. Because only a few hundred years after the flood, this corruption spread again with Sodom where there was only one righteous man, Lot. As a result, Two angels came to rescue Lot and his family from the impending judgment.

"Lot, who was oppressed by the filthy conduct of the wicked, tormented his righteous soul from day to day by seeing and hearing their lawless deeds." 2 Peter 2:7

"As Sodom and Gomorrah and the cities around them, having given themselves over to sexual immorality and gone after strange flesh, are set forth as an example suffering the vengeance of eternal fire." Jude 7

"Then the Lord rained brimstone and fire on Sodom and Gomorrah from the Lord out of the Heavens. He overthrew those cities, all the plain, all the inhibitors of the cities, and what grew on the ground." Genesis 19:23

Jesus said, "as it was in the days of Lot, even thus shall it be in the day when the Son of Man is revealed. They eat, drink, bought and sold, but the same day Lot went out of Sodom, it rained fire and brimstone from heaven, and destroyed them all." Luke 17:29

TWO ARKS

Noah's Ark

"The divine long suffering waited in the days of Noah while the ark was being prepared in which a few, that is, eight souls were saved through water." Peter 3:20

Noah being a just man, manifested his faith when warned about things not yet seen and in holy fear built an ark. As a preacher of righteousness, Noah tried to prepare his generation proclaiming the truth for 120 years, living in a manner pleasing to God and being perfect in his generations. Noah had announced a coming judgment and offered a way to escape from it but the people ignored it and were swept away in the judgment. The ark had only one door in it which symbolized hope and salvation as Jesus said,

"I am the door, by me if any enter in he shall be saved." John 10:9

As long as the ark door remained open, deliverance from judgment was an option. Gods' provision was offered and the way of escape was available. Only those who entered the ark by faith were saved from the flood and those who enter the heavenly ark through the door of faith in Jesus Christ are saved for eternity. The ark was Gods' provision for Noah as Christ is Gods provision for sinners. Noah, as a type of Christ illustrates how salvation works, all who were joined to Noah were saved from the impending disaster. A reproduction of the days of Noah will be the characteristics of a world when Christ returns as he said;

"For as in the days that were before the flood, they were eating and drinking, marrying and given in marriage until the day that Noah entered into the ark, and knew not until the flood came, and took them all away, so shall also the coming of the Son of Man be." Matthew 24:37

Jesus indicated that just as God's judgement came upon the unsaved in Noah's time <u>in the day</u> Noah entered the ark and <u>on the day</u> Lot went out of Sodom, so God's judgement will come again upon the unsaved on the earth <u>in the day</u> when the Son of man is revealed.

The Ark Of The Covenant

"O ark of God, thou precious ark, all who know you will seek after you, and worship before you."   2 Chronicles 5:9

Here we see Two in regards to the cherubims upon the ark guarding Gods' throne. Representing the very throne of God on earth beneath the wings of guarding cherubim, God poured forth his mercy.

The ark was the center of the tabernacle and signified God's presence, law, covenant, mercy and testimony. This was where God met man and would speak from the mercy seat merging time, space and eternity at one place. The most important part of the ark is that it represented Jesus Christ and typified how grace is given to us through Christ. Now mankind has been given access to the presence of God through Christ Jesus our high priest. Having Christ, we have the presence of God with us so we must keep him center in our lives, just as the ark was the center of the tabernacle. Remember Gods purpose, design and desire has always been to dwell among his people and commune with them.

TWO CALLINGS

"I am the Lord that brought thee out of Ur of the Chaldees, to give thee this land to inherit" Genesis 15:7

To accomplish his grand design and illustrate his divine sovereignty, the Lord sent Abraham to the land of Moriah to test his faith. Abraham journeyed to the land of Moriah where the angel of the Lord called out to him from heaven Two times to withhold him from sacrificing his only son Isaac. Abraham was also told Two times that he would inherit the land of Canaan.

"In the same day, the Lord made a covenant with Abram saying unto thy seed have I given this land." Genesis 15:18

Abraham became the physical father of the Jewish people and the spiritual father of the church. Two separate and distinct lines of descendants.

Another interesting occurrence of this number is when Isaacs's wife was pregnant, the Lord said to her:

"Two nations are in thy womb, and Two manners of people shall be separated from thy bowels and the one people shall be stronger than the other people, and the elder shall serve the younger." Genesis 25:23

One of the prominent and divine dealings was with Jacob, for he had Two wives, Two concubines, Two handmaids, Two woman servants, and Two names.

"And God said unto him thy name is Jacob; thy name shall not be called Jacob, but Israel shall be thy name and he called him Israel."
Genesis 35:10

Jacob was the second born of twins which represents the second birth.

Joseph and Pharaoh both had Two dreams which were but the instrument employed by God to accomplish his purposes.

"For these Two years hath famine been in the land and God sent me before you to preserve you a posterity in the earth and to save your lives by a great deliverance." Genesis 45:7

Joseph is by far the most outstanding type of Jesus, he became a servant, overcame temptation, was falsely accused, condemned with Two criminals, rejected by his own brethren, and exalted to be a prince. Eventually, he was made known to his brethren the second time. God chose Moses and Aaron as his Two witnesses to Pharaoh.

"Two are better than one because they have a good reward for their labor." Ecclesiastes 4:9

Moses received Two signs of authority which were used against Pharaoh's Two Magicians.

"And it shall come to pass, if they will not also believe these Two signs, the water out of the river shall become blood upon the dry land." Exodus 2:13

After leaving Egypt and journeying through the wilderness, Moses was instructed to come up to Mt. Sinai to receive the law.

TWO MOUNTAINS

Mt. Horeb

"I will stand there before you by the rock at Horeb. Strike the rock, and water will come out of it for the people to drink." Exodus 17:6

Appearing first in Exodus 3:1 and continuing seventeen more times, this mountain is referenced as holy ground and also means desert. Josephus claims it's the highest of all mountains, errible and inaccessible and cannot be looked at without painness of the eyes. Sometimes called the mountain of God, this is where Moses struck the rock and Elijah escaped from Jezebel.

"And the Lord said to Aaron, go into the wilderness to meet Moses, and he went and met him in the mountain of God and kissed him." Exodus 4:27

Mt. Sinai

"Now Mount Sinai was wrapped in smoke because the Lord had descended on it in fire. The smoke of it went up like the smoke of a kiln, and the whole mountain trembled greatly."
Exodus 19:18

Sinai means to shine, as we note the glory of Yahweh was like a devouring fire on top of the mountain. Used 21 times, this mountain had a transit function in Israel's pilgrimage. As a mountain of transition, God appeared in person and gave Moses the law. This is where Israel entered into a covenant relationship, became a nation and were called to be holy and separated from the nation's surrounding them.

TWO TABLETS

"And he gave unto Moses Two tablets of testimony, tablets of stone, written with the finger of God." Exodus 31:18

A deeper truth of this number is hidden within the pages of scripture regarding the Two sets of tablets. God's holy righteous commandments were written on Two tablets of stone signifying the condition of their hearts at the time. He gave them commandments signifying his direct authority. This first set was smashed on the rocks when Moses came down from the mountain and witnessed how quickly the people had turned back to Egypt. A second set of tablets like the first had to be made because of Israel's unfaithfulness.

They are a witness to the rejection of God's perfect law. God's testimony stands on the Two tablets of the law, hence the testimony is the law. On God's side, it's testimony but on the human side, it's law. The law testifies to what God requires and demands. The law is the revelation of Gods' will and became Israels wisdom and understanding.

"Lo, I come to do thy will of God, he taketh away the first, that he may establish the second." Hebrews 10:9

This also foreshadows how they will receive the Messiah the second time. Moses striking the rock Two times may also signify this. The typology of the rock represents Christ who will only go to the cross once to die and that's all that's needed for atonement and salvation. A picture of the Messiah the rock of our salvation. Speaking refers to faith and the water represents eternal life, so we are to believe then speak to the rock by faith and ask for salvation.

Moses is instructed to build the Tabernacle of the Testimony which held the law inside. On the top of the ark were Two cherubims reflecting God's grace and mercy. This tabernacle would be enclosed within Two veils.

TWO VEILS

First Veil

"Behold the veil of the temple was rent in Two, from the top to the bottom, and the earth did quake and the rocks rent." Matthew 27:51

A wondrous proof of the divine inspiration of the word of God in relation to this number is revealed in the tabernacle. Just as there were Two veils in the earthly tabernacle, so there are Two veils in the spiritual realm. The veils between Heaven and Earth are a protective barrier modeled for us by the Tabernacle representing the physical and spiritual. God's desire has always been to dwell with men openly without any kind of veil where the terrestrial realm and the spiritual realm are one.

The first veil was the entrance into the compound of the **tabernacle**. The second veil represented the flesh of Jesus that was ripped from top to bottom signifying the reconciliation of all things to himself.

Only by passing through the rent veil of Christ's flesh can we enter into the Holy of Holies to approach and worship God based solely on his sons blood.

"Seeing then we have a great high priest that has passed into the heavens, Jesus the son of God." Hebrews 4:14

This was also a public sign of God rejecting and ending the Levitical priesthood. God no longer required animal sacrifices in order to have access to the Holy of Holies, any such further sacrifices would be rejected because Jesus was the final sacrifice.

Second Veil

Presently, the new and living way into the Holy of Holies is found through a relationship with Jesus, not through a physical temple. Behind the second veil was the **Holy of Holies** where the ark was. When Jesus returns the second time showing and declaring himself king, he will be publicly presented as the son of God. Currently, a veil lies over the hearts of the Jewish people, and we must pray so they can see and have hope in the one true Messiah.

This pattern of Twos continues for the Israelites with the offering of Two lambs, Two wave loaves, and Two goats.

TWO GOATS

First Goat (Forgiven)

"And he shall take the Two goats and present them before the Lord at the door to the tabernacle of the congregation." Leviticus 16:7

The first goat was for the Lord as a sin offering to make atonement in the holy place for the children of Israel once a year.

"For on that day shall the priest make atonement for you, to cleanse you that ye may be clean from all your sins before the Lord." Leviticus 17:30

This goat was killed and burned on the altar. And his blood was sprinkled on the ark thus asking God to forgive the sins of the people.

Second Goat (Forgotten)

The second goat was a scapegoat. The priest would confess over it all the iniquities and transgressions, putting them on the head of the goat and sending it away into the wilderness. This goat banished the sins of the Israelites to the outside of the camp because inside was holy ground. This showed the sins of the people were taken away never to come back to them.

The purpose of the Two goats was to show the people's sins were forgiven and forgotten.

TWO LAWS

The Old

`"Having abolished in his flesh the enmity, even the law of commandments contained in ordinances for to make in himself of Twain one new man, so making peace and that he might reconcile both unto God in one body by the cross having slain the enmity thereby." Ephesians 2:15

The law itself looks forward through the sacrifices to a salvation which they foreshadowed. The law only brought sin to light and proved that for righteousness there was a need for the work of Christ. The law was for a standard of conduct not as the ground for justification. The old law brings the knowledge of sin and defines it and displays the standards of God. The law of sin and death convicts, condemns, and reveals sin. The law was given to expose the nature of man. Our righteousness could never satisfy the demands of the law, it was designed to magnify our real condition before God. Since the law is established in letter and not in the Holy Spirit, it causes man to die. Without the spirit, the word of God becomes a dead letter. Whatever is of the Holy Spirit is by

faith and one must have faith to receive the truth.
Sacrifices in the Old Testament could not fully take
away the sins of the people, they were done for
ceremonial purification, and to point forward to
Jesus the one and only perfect sacrifice for sins.
Sin is not only an influence and power but it's also
a law, and the law of sin brings us into captivity. All
man's will cannot conquer this. Man's power
cannot overcome natural law, thus the law was to
show us what sin is, provoke us to sin the more
until we are forced to admit we have a sin problem
and a need for a savior. The law shows us our sin
and points us to the marvelous grace of Christ who
is the end of the law. Grace means that God does
something for me and the law means that I do
something for God. Trying to do something for
God places me under the law. The death of Jesus
has forever freed us from the law.

The New

"Now the righteousness of God without the law is manifested being witnessed by the law and the prophets which is by faith of Jesus Christ unto all that believe." Romans 3:21

The spirit of life is also a law, thereby this law we are made free from the law of sin and death. This law overcomes the first law for us, in us, converting the soul.

Through co-death, we are set free from the law of sin. By co-resurrection, we are delivered from the law of death. The cross broke down the separation of Jew and Gentile reconciling them back to God in one body. The cross abolished the covenant and the curse of the law. We are now ambassadors of Christ submitting to the word of Christ having the mind and authority of Christ. The deliverance of God wrought by Moses was only a physical deliverance and the law was external. Again a type and shadow of the spiritual deliverance the Messiah would provide giving a new nature being born again by the incorruptible seed of God.

TWO STONES

"And thou shalt take Two onyx stones and grave on them the names of the children of Israel." Exodus 28:9

The Israelites sometimes consulted the Urim and Thummim to receive answers to their questions. In the Old Testament, God spoke to the high priest in a few instances by the way of Urim and Thummim. These Two items are known as lights and perfections and were used to decipher God's will. The priest would wear them behind the breastplate close to the heart. These Two hidden pieces would give the yes or no they were seeking. This was the way to receive witness from God, which correlates to the Holy Spirit within our hearts today. Spirit led living trusting the inner witness of the Holy Spirit.

"The Holy Spirit only bears witness to the truth, because the spirit is truth." John 5:6

We find both design and significance of the number Two associated with the breast Plate. Upon the chest of Christ hangs the Urim and Thummim and you will find direction from him in every difficulty and dilemma.

TWO TRUMPETS

"Make the Two trumpets of silver of a whole piece shalt thou make them that thou mayest use them for the calling of the assembly and for the journeyings of the camps." Numbers 10:2

These trumpets have many meanings like gathering, departure, proclamation, or alarm. As Gods Two groups of witnesses, both Israel and the church are also the Lord's trumpets.

Israel announced the existence of God, had a physical origin in him and were to reflect him to the world. Israel was called to be a living testimony of God given the role of being a light to the nations. Unbelievers need to see the love of God before they are ready to hear about the love of God. The church continues its mandate of spreading the Gospel accurately representing the truth of Salvation through Jesus Christ and announcing his return.

The Trump of God

The first Trump of God called the people together to be placed under the law or the ministry of death. By contrast the purpose of the last T.O.G. will be to call the people to Christ and abolish the last enemy death. Because sin causes death and the strength of sin is the law. The first T.O.G. was for the giving of this ministry and the last T.O.G. will be sounded in conjunction with the rapture and its signal is the beginning of the end for death.

In summoning the dead to life and the living to immortality, it seems that the contrast between the first T.O.G and the last T.O.G. are related. As spiritual death and spiritual life and physical death and resurrection.

God always validates his Word by being witnessed by Two. Moses would send men to search out the land of Canaan in which only Two would bring back in a good report and be allowed in. Joshua sent Two men to spy on Jericho. Samuel would anoint Two men to become king, Saul who would reign for Two years, and David whose throne would never end. Solomon, David's son, proved God's wisdom when Two harlots disputed about a child and he said to divide the child in Two. God had also appeared to Solomon in Two dreams, and granted both wisdom and understand-ing to him. With this knowledge, Solomon built the temple sanctuary which had Two doors, Two panels, and Two pillars which had Two networks, Two rows of pomegranates, and Two capitals.

TWO TEMPLES

First Temple

The first temple was built by Solomon and signified that God and his people dwelt together. Glorious and elaborate this temple was used for ceremony and sacrifice. The site chosen by David was on top of Mt. Moriah where Abraham was willing to offer his son. Taking seven years to complete followed by seven days of inaugural celebrations. Here the divine presence was manifest, God's glory dwelling in the physical world. This was the heart and center of worship until 587 when it was destroyed.

Second Temple

The second temple was repaired and completed by the Gentiles in 515 B.C., but unfortunately it was a dim reflection of the former glory of the first temple and did not have the ark of the covenant. Both temples suffered through neglect and were destroyed on the self-same day. The Old Testament period had a central temple for worship, but in the New Testament, there is no physical building.

Believers as the body of Christ, are the spiritual temple. Just as the tabernacle in the wilderness was a type and shadow of our new covenant realties, being covered in flesh allowing God to dwell in the midst and the Holy Spirit to move into the heart of the believer. The spiritual temple grows with each new member added to the church through the new birth. Those who believe in Christ are born again and become lively stones. The Lord offered himself as a sacrifice, abolishing the earthly temple so as to draw men to worship him.

"For under the new covenant, we are to worship God in spirit and truth." John 4:23

After years of rebellion and unfaithfulness, God punished Israel, splitting up the kingdom and sending them into exile. Here we see the number Two is used again for <u>division</u>.

"For my people have committed Two evils, they have forsaken me the fountain of living waters and hewed cisterns that can hold no water." Jeremiah 2:13

The house of Judah formed the southern kingdom with Two tribes and the house of Israel formed the northern kingdom with ten tribes. The northern kingdom was conquered and exiled by Assyria and came to be known as the lost tribes of Israel. The nation of Israel was no longer a state or country. Their refusal to heed to God and the demands of the kingship lead to their fall, despite all the prophets sent to them.

Again, orchestrated by God Nebuchadnezzar had Two dreams and Daniel had Two visions which were explained to him by Two angels. Another angel communed with Zechariah showing him Two olive trees on either side of a candlestick that had Two golden pipes. He is told that these are the Two anointed ones who stand by the Lord of the whole Earth. Then he is shown Two women carrying an ephah and Two mountains of brass. As promised in the Old Testament God sends his Son the Messiah.

"The Lord thy God will raise up unto thee a prophet from the mist of thee of thy brethren like unto me, unto him ye shall hearken."
Deuteronomy 18:15

Jesus did not bear the corrupted flesh of all other people in history because He was not begotten of Adam. He was the only begotten Son of God, his spiritual nature was holy divine.

There were Two people who gave witness and testimony to this at his dedication that in fact, Jesus is the promised Messiah. Simeon said,

"Lord now lettest thou thy servant depart in peace according to thy word, for mine eyes have seen thy salvation." Luke 2:29

And Anna a prophetess, "coming in that instant gave thanks likewise unto the Lord, and spoke of him to them that looked for redemption in Jerusalem." Luke 2:38

ALSO;

"It is also written in your law that the testimony of Two is true. I am one that bears witness of myself and the Father that sent me beareth witness of me." John 8:16

Jehovah of the Old Testament now becomes Jesus of the New Testament. At his baptism, the Father and the Holy Ghost are present to reveal that Jesus is God's son.

"And Lo a voice from heaven saying this is my beloved son in whom I am well pleased." Matthew 3:17

"John too gave witness saying I saw the Spirit descending from heaven like a dove and it abode upon him." John 1:32

"And straight away coming up out of the water he saw heaven opened and the spirit like a dove descending upon him." Mark 1:10

Here we see the union of the son and the holy spirit, Two is one.

TWO PURPOSES

The first coming of Jesus did not bring peace but <u>division.</u> At his second advent He will bring peace. As the <u>second</u> person of the Godhead Jesus is both God and man. As both human and divine Christ partakes of the attributes of both natures so that whatever is true of either nature is true of the one person. A human divine <u>union</u> the person of Christ, one infinite and one finite truly God and truly man simultaneously. The Two natures are united without mixture and maintain their separate Identities without transfer of one nature to the other. Embracing humanity made him no less God and retaining deity did not make him less human. These natures remain distinct as the human nature always remained human and the divine nature always remained divine. Christ had to operate within the human sphere to accomplish his earthly purpose according to the eternal plan of salvation. At the same time, he operated in the divine sphere to the extent that it was possible. Jesus became a man in order to redeem man. Christ in his humanity is presented as the son of man, Jesus Christ his earthly name. As the son of God Christ Jesus is the name of his resurrection, hence we can only be in Christ. We are actively United with him in his resurrection by his spirit, because God had joined us to him.

"But of him are ye in Christ Jesus."
Corinthians 1:30

As the son of God, his deity is crystal clear revolving around seven miracles and I am statements in order to engender believing faith. The dual purpose of his agenda is to bring his gospel of redemption by grace and to establish his rightful righteous rule. A great plan of salvation and a kingdom for his rule of law. His life of service and sacrifice was to atone for sin and restore all creation back to God. Jesus functioning in Two different roles at Two different times will come back to set up his kingdom. As the conquering king Jesus will rule and restore David's kingdom providing reconciliation and reunion of the Two houses of Israel with his sovereignty being fully manifested on Earth. Jesus, who responded to the will of the father, as a sacrifice, was obedient even to death, and now is our high priest and king. As our high priest, he reaches into the heart to minister and restores the sinful state of man. Jesus was baptized into the priesthood, and anointed with the Holy Spirit to become our high priestly king in the order of the Melchizedek.

"The Lord Jesus is the Christ of God as well as the son of God. He has been made both Lord and Christ by God." Acts 2:36

The first time the Lord Jesus was seen by his brethren after the flesh they knew him not, but when they see him the second time, he shall be known by them. There was a symbolic significance in the fact that Jesus sent his disciples forth Two by Two. Combined they have a deeper testimony of victory found in the Lord.

"For where Two are gathered together in my name there I am in the midst of them."
Matthew 18:20

"Can Two walk together, except they be agreed." Amos 3:3

Most of Jesus' parables came in Twos, such as Two coins, Two mites, Two sparrows, Two masters, Two talents, Two debaters, Two coats, Two sons, and Two praying. He also gave Two great commandments.

TWO COMMANDMENTS

"The first of all the commandments, hear O Israel the Lord our God is one and thou shalt love the Lord thy God with all thy heart and with all thy soul, and with all thy mind and with all thy strength, this is the first commandment."
Mark 12:29

The First

Jesus summarizes the entire law with love for God and your neighbor and says on these Two commandments hang all the law and prophets. God desires absolute exclusivity, we cannot be unfaithful with spiritual adultery having our minds on anything other than him.

"No man can serve Two masters, for either he will hate the one, and love the other or else he will hold to the one and despise the other."
Matthew 6:24

The Second

"Thou shall love the Lord thy God with all thy heart and with all thy soul and with all thy mind and thou shall love thy neighbor as thyself."
Matthew 22:40

And the second is namely this, thou shalt love thy neighbor as thyself. So the first one includes all the commandments which are in relation to God, and the second one all those pertaining to man. He who loves his neighbor fulfills all the commandments and he who fulfills all the commandments loves God. Both lead us into spiritual growth and communion with God and fellow beings. As we love others we are loving God because all were made in the image of God. Jesus who is the embodiment of love is our example of how we should treat others. Laying down his life he demonstrated his perfect love for humanity.

TWO COVENANTS

"But before faith came, we were kept under the law shut up unto faith which should afterwards be revealed." Galatians 3:23

The Old

The old covenant or age of Torah, could point out and condemn the guilty, but couldn't fix the problem. It was only a physical deliverance. The law confronts imperfect man with a perfect standard that exposes his inner defect of sin. Therefore, being external the law could only be a schoolmaster to bring believers to something better.

The old covenant is a lifeless code of moral demands that prepares us to receive Christ by faith who has abolished this covenant of sacred rites with the new covenant through his blood. These covenant sacrifices demonstrated faith and obedience in following the commandments but have now been annulled through the finished work of Jesus.

The New

"…for Christ is the end of the law to everyone who believes." Romans 10:4

The promises of the Abrahamic covenant are the foundations of the new covenant. These promises are to all nations by grace through faith in Jesus. This new covenant or age of grace could now fix and reconcile us back to God. The new covenant was made effective through the sinless sacrifice of Jesus on calvary's cross. Throughout the completed works of Jesus the Holy Spirit now writes the law of God on our hearts. The new covenant is an eternal unconditional covenant based solely on the shedding blood of Christ. With the promise of the Holy Spirit which provides a new heart and mind we can now know and love God. Jesus Christ has made the new covenant of salvation to all who will believe. Grace is the principle on which God justifies a sinner, faith is the principle on which the benefit is received. We are justified freely by his grace through the redemption that is in Christ Jesus. The unique difference between the old and new covenant is made visible in Israel and the church. The regeneration and justification of Israel waits for this future fulfillment being literal and unconditional.

Another interesting occurrence of this number is when Jesus appeared with Two prophets on a mountain and reveals a glimpse of his glory at the transfiguration with Moses and Elijah. Jesus also sent Two disciples ahead to retrieve a colt for him to ride on. He sent Two disciples to prepare a room for the Passover meal, and there were Two false witnesses at his trial and Two criminals crucified with him.

"Then there were Two thieves crucified with him, one on the right hand and another on the left." Matthew 27:38

"And seeth Two angels in white sitting, the one at the head, and the other at the feet, where the body of Jesus had lain." John 20:12

God validates the resurrection in Luke by Two witnesses traveling to Emmaus and talking to the risen Christ.

"After that he appeared in another form unto Two of them as they walked and went into the country." Mark 16:2

So Jesus doesn't leave us without assurances, God's oaths and promises hold us securely in the faith.

"That by which Two immutable things in which is impossible for God to lie." Hebrews 6:18

This purpose is to bring comfort, guidance, and encouragement. He has pledged the honor of his name and our security depends far more on God holding on to us and fulfilling his promise and oath. What God has promised is sure and what God has done fully confirms it.

TWO ROCKS

Rock of Offense

"Behold I lay in Sion a stumbling block and rock of offense and whosoever believeth on him shall not be ashamed." Romans 9:33

This stone symbolically represents the second person of the trinity God the son, the Lord Jesus the Messiah. This signifies that salvation is by grace through faith by Jesus apart from works of the law.

"This is the stone which is set at naught of you builders which is become the head of the corner." Acts 4:11

Trying to attain righteousness by works coupled with the rejection of the messiah proved to be the twofold attitude of stumbling and offense. For Israel the gospel of Christ was an offense because it set aside religion. The Jews ignorance also concluded that God intended to save them only and were offended at this and did not obtain it. "Whosoever shall fall on this stone shall be broken but on whomsoever it shall fall it will grind him to powder." Matthew 21:44

Stumbling Block

"But we preach Christ crucified, unto the Jews a stumbling block." Corinthians 1:23

Israel failed to obtain righteousness because they tried to obtain it by the works of the law. They had a zeal for God, but not according to knowledge. They failed to distinguish between faith and legal and were ignorant that Jesus was the Messiah and the end of the law. They tried to establish their own righteousness which is not attainable by human effort, rather faith and belief is the only way. Israel failed to submit to the gospel message, because faith comes by hearing and hearing by the word of God.

"For Christ is the end of the law for righteousness to everyone that believeth."
Romans 10:4

In spite of this, God has not cast off his people, for there is always a remanent that comes to saving faith.

"But Israel shall be saved in the Lord with an everlasting salvation." Isaiah 45:17

TWO GOSPELS

The Gospel of the Kingdom

"I must preach the Kingdom of God to other cities also, for therefore am I sent." Luke 4:43

This message was preached by Jesus and his disciples up until Israel committed the unpardonable national sin in rejecting him as the Messiah.

"The kingdom of God shall be taken from you and given to a nation bringing forth fruits thereof." Matthew 21:43

The Gospel of Grace

"For by grace you. have been saved through faith and that not of yourselves, it is the gift of God." Ephesians 2:8

This Gospel was preached by Paul who received it by real revelation through the risen Lord. Salvation had been accomplished, Gods grace was now being bestowed on those who believed. The Gospel of grace teaches that Jesus died for our sins, was buried and rose agin on the third day according to the scriptures. When the age of grace comes to a close, God will then turn his attention back to the nation of Israel.

TWO BIRTHS

"He that is joined unto the Lord is one spirit. For Two saith he shall be one flesh."
1 Corinthians 6:16.

Our first natural birth comes when we enter into this world. Sin was introduced by Satan the originator of rebellion and sin causing the fall of creation. Now we live in subject to the influence of sin with an inherit and genetic predisposition of ungodly values and character traits.

Our second supernatural birth comes as we are baptized by the spirit into the body of Christ. Regeneration is the supernatural operation of God. In this new birth we are made partakers of the divine nature in receiving God's own life. The new birth is an act of creative power, the impartation of spiritual life, and the communication to us of the divine nature itself. This makes us a member of his holy family, having become united with him by his death. We are united with him also by the likeness of his resurrection. A baptism into the death of Christ ends our relationship with the old world and resurrection brings us into this new one. The grace of God abolished the division between Jew and

Gentile to bring about the unity of the spirit in those who believe.

"For this cause shall a man leave his wife, and they Two shall be one flesh speak concerning Christ and the church." Ephesians 5:31

The new birth is due to the sovereign will of the Father, Son, and the Holy Spirit. The father predestinates it, the son propitiates it, and the spirit regenerates us. All three are concerned with our salvation. The cause of election must always be traced to God's will. Election itself is of grace therefore it depends in no wise upon any worthiness. If it did it would no longer be grace. God's choice is not determined by any good or merit with ourselves, but it is all sovereign gratuitous grace undeserved and unmerited favor. The eternal purpose of God is foreordained for us to be conformed in the image of his son. May this Divine grace enable us to walk by faith and not by sight as pilgrims separate from the world in unreserved obedience submitting to the will of God. At the new birth, God's spirit comes to rest within the new creation and so we are filled and born again.

"They Twain shall be one flesh, what therefore God has joined together let no man put asunder." Matthew 19:6

Just as God created man in his own image and likeness so the Christ in me leads to I in Christ being renewed in the knowledge according to his image. At the new birth, we are placed in Christ and God restores the believer.

"Being born again not of corruptible seed but incorruptible by the word of God which lives and abides forever." 1 Peter 1:23

The Lord in his infinite mercy dropped his divine life into us, the living incorruptible seed that abides forever. As Christ was born of the Spirit so is the new man. A living union with Christ through personal faith in him as our savior. The mystery of godliness is Christ living through the believer having the character of Christ and the fruits of the new birth which are holiness and righteousness. God does something for us, in order to do something in us, so he can flow through us.

There's also a twofold redemption: one for the body, one for the soul.

"Whom he justified, them he also glorified."
Romans 8:30

The Holy Spirit not only witnesses to salvation but he guarantees the redemption of the body. Regeneration is wrought by the word of God and the spirit of God.

"Accept a man be born of water and of the spirit, he cannot enter the kingdom of God."
John 3:5

Water referring to the word. The believer is born again, created a new, made alive and passed out of death into life. The spirit works through the word and the new birth is the impartation of a new nature. The new birth is a reception of a life altogether new that through the cross of our Lord Jesus Christ the old life/world has been crucified and by the resurrection a new creation has been brought in.

TWO NATURES

The Old

"That which is born of the flesh is flesh; and that which is born of the Spirit is spirit." John 3:6

The old nature is generated by our five carnal senses which are all a part of the flesh. The old nature does not conform to God's standard and has no fellowship with the divine. The flesh is the earthly nature of man that is apart from God's influence, prone to sin, and opposed to God. Inclined to fill pleasurable desires it gratifies the carnal appetites. This animalistic nature incited to sin leads to the manifestations of the flesh. Human nature cannot change, it must die.

The cross is the instrument by which we crucify the flesh and the Holy Spirit is the power by which we keep the flesh from resurrecting. The cross and the Holy Spirit are the Two ways to overcome the flesh. We are to reckon ourselves dead to the flesh and walk by the spirit. An unregenerated soulish man does not have the spirit and lacks the faculty to know God's word and receive revelation from God.

Sin is a living fallen nature, nothing more than a beast. Sin reigning in the body becomes man's nature enslaving the soul compelling it to walk after sin contrary to God. Living in this nature caters to impulses of the flesh to fulfill pleasurable desires that gratify carnal appetites. As with the physical death, sin is the cause of our spiritual death, it's what separates us from God who is the source of life. After we have been born again we will begin to naturally walk after the spirit, not to fulfill the lust of the flesh.

The New

The Two natures are distinct and diverse and in an open antagonism the one to the other. This conflict within is the proof of the Two natures residing. It's not until the believer receives the new nature that he discovers the real character of the old. For the unregenerate man is blind to the vileness of the flesh. Our new nature is regenerated and created after the image of God in righteousness and true holiness. The basic prerequisite for this is to follow the spirit and live under its power and walk according to the spirit. We can now renew the mind to know and prove the acceptable will of God. God gives us this new nature after we have believed in the Lord Jesus Christ. Now filled with the Holy Spirit we begin to grow the fruit of the spirit in our lives. God manifested his grace through Jesus to provide salvation from the old nature, and the righteousness of Christ is imputed to all believers. We lose our soulish fleshy life to inherit eternal life.

The corrupt nature from birth is neither removed or refined but remains and opposes the new. One in submission to God, the other in rebellion against him. The one contrary to the other, the flesh and the spirit, Two capacities within the believer, the old man, of flesh, and the new man the spirit. Despite this inner battle we are to regard the flesh as once and for all dead and walk in spirit. Positionally the flesh is dead, but experimentally it still struggles for supremacy. Being reconstituted and restored to walk in the spirit not to fulfill the lust of the flesh, we take on the character and mind of God living by faith so that Christ in me is the hope of glory. Salvation is not a work of man for God, but a work of God for man. It depends completely upon divine grace without respect to human merit. Christ in dwelling the believer in the sense of eternal life living in union by the baptism of the spirit.

TWO REALMS

The Fleshly

"Now the natural man receiveth not the things of the spirit of God, he is unable to comprehend spiritual things for they are foolishness unto him, neither can he know them because they are spiritually discerned." 1 Corinthians 2:14

The unregenerate natural man is void of Gods spirit and incapable of understanding God's will. Alienated from God he maintains a strong will and is prideful and emotional. This nature does not conform to God's standard and has no fellowship with the divine. The action of the will is determined by the condition of the mind, regulated by its sinful nature. Any thought, word, or action is generated and motivated by the flesh. This soul power is a latent force of the fallen man bound by the flesh and is all vanity, being independent, proud, and self-centered.

The Spiritual

"It is the spirit that quickeneth, the flesh profiteth nothing, the words that I speak unto you, they are spirit and they are life." John 6:63

The words spoken by our Lord were life-giving but to the unbelieving they became flesh. For the word of God is spirit and he has revealed it through the spirit.

The words as revealed and taught by the Holy Spirit are the words of wisdom and revelation. We must possess the nature of God to have a relationship with him. The spirit is life-giving, it's Christs' presence within us to show forth his son in us.

"We have received not the spirit of the world, but the spirit which is from God, that we might know the things that were freely given to us by God." 1 Corinthians 2:12

TWO DAYS

The Day of Christ

The day of Christ is <u>that day</u> and relates to the church's translation, glorification, and examination for reward.

"But ye brethren are not in darkness that <u>that day</u> should overtake you as a thief."
1 Thessalonians 5:4

"And to you who are troubled rest with us when the Lord Jesus shall Come to be glorified in his saints in <u>that day</u>." 2 Thessalonians

"And take heed to yourselves, lest at any time your hearts be overcharged with surfeiting and darkness and cares of this life, and so <u>that day</u> come upon you unawares, for as a snare shall it come on all them that dwell on the face of the whole Earth."
Luke 21:34

The Day of the Lord

"He hath appointed a day in the which he will judge the world in righteousness by that man whom he hath ordained." Acts 17:31

The day of the Lord is connected with judgments and events related to the second advent at the beginning of the tribulation after the rapture and extending through to the coming of our Lord unto the millennium.

This judgment includes not only specific judgments upon Israel but also the nations during the tribulation cumulating with the son of God coming to claim the world for which he died and exerting his power and authority over it. Jesus will exercise his rule in visible form over the whole world, restoring his theocratic kingdom on earth.

"Beloved, be not ignorant of this one thing, that one day is with the Lord as 1000 years and a 1000 years as one day." 2 Peter 3:8

TWO STAGES

For His Saints

"Then we which are alive and remain shall be caught up together with them in the clouds to meet the Lord in the air and so shall ever be with the Lord." 1 Thessalonians 4:17

The church, which is bound up in the spirit will meet Jesus in the air and the earth will no longer be our residence. Just as with Pentecost the church was instantly created so to in the twinkling of an eye shall the church be taken up. Thus, the believer is longing to be clothed with immortality because this kind of body with its sin nature cannot enter into the eternal state. A translation will be necessary before we can enter the kingdom of God. A change from corruption to incorruption and from mortality to immortality. The redemption of our body.

"And as we have born the image of the earthly, we shall also bear the image of the heaven." 1 Corinthians 15:49

With His Saints

"Behold the Lord cometh with ten thousandths of his saints to execute judgement." Jude 14

Jesus returns to earth to reveal himself to all humanity with his saints at the end of the seven years of judgement for the battle of Armageddon. The second advent of Christ coming to earth will begin with every eye seeing him and all kindreds of the earth shall wail because of him.

"Wail for the day of the Lord is near, it will come like destruction from the Almighty." Isaiah 13:6

Only after Israel's faith producing repentance will God send his son back to earth to reign and the times of refreshing will come and his kingdom will be established.

TWO WIVES

The Bride of Christ

"For Two shall be one flesh, this is a great mystery but I speak concerning Christ in the church." Ephesians 5:32

The church comprised of the union of both Jew and Gentile being the body of Christ was a great mystery. A body of divine knowledge that was kept completely hidden in ages past which now has been revealed. The church as part of God's eternal plan in eternity past would come into existence as a result of Christ's death. This mystery in the past was hidden in God, but now the believers are hidden in God. Christ indwelling all the believers which is the hope of Glory. The mystery of the disposition of grace is to witness that in fact all Jewish and Gentile believers are united together in one body.

"And to make all men see what is the fellowship of the mystery which from the beginning of the world has been hid in God who created all things by Jesus Christ." Ephesians 3:9

Gentile believers now enjoy the spiritual blessings and are grafted into a Jewish olive tree.

The church is betrothed but not yet joined to her husband but will be presented as a pure virgin at her union with the messiah. Jesus proved his love for the church by dying for her, that he might sanctify her. Jesus purchased the church and will come back for her at the rapture.

The Wife of Jehovah

"Jehovah your God has chosen you to be a people for his own possession above all peoples that are upon the face of the earth." Deuteronomy 7:6

Israel, the wife of God the father was chosen to enter into a covenant and in this relationship was the marriage contract. Because of adultery, the marriage contract was broken and a bill of divorce was issued as we see in Hosea and Jeremiah. However, the prophets declare that God has promised to restore and provide for Israel like a husband with the new covenant. God will enter into a new and everlasting covenant with Israel in the future.

TWO RAPTURES

"By faith Enoch was translated that he should not see death, and was not found because God had took him, for before his translation he had this testimony that he pleased God." Hebrews 11:5

"Enoch"

Enoch can be viewed as a type of the rapture of the church leaving without dying, taken up before the judgment came. Faith was the instrument and because of his testimony that pleased God we know without faith it is impossible to please God. Thus, saved by grace through faith Enoch was made a partaker of the divine and taken up. Enoch conforming to and walking with God passed through the portals of death and went to Heaven. The rapture or translation is our transformation into the image of him who was transformed before us. We must walk with God before we can witness for God. To walk indicates fellowship, friendship and denotes unity of purpose to glorify God. We walk before God as children, we walk after him as servants, we walk with him as friends, and walk in him as members of his body. Enoch was a supreme witness for God walking in fellowship manifesting his glory. As a type of those believers who shall be likewise caught up illustrating to us how we must walk in spiritual communion, absolute dependency, surrendered will and faith.

"Elijah"

"And it came to pass as they still went on and talked that behold there appeared a chariot of fire and horse of fire, and parted them both asunder and Elijah went up by a whirlwind into Heaven."
2 Kings 2:11

Elijah too is also a type of the translated saints. John the Baptist came in the spirit and power of Elijah to make ready a people prepared for the Lord. This time Elijah himself will come to prepare people for the Lords' second coming.

"Behold I will send Elijah the prophet before the coming of the great and dreadful day of the Lord." Malachi 4:5

As an instantaneous unannounced event that will happen in a twinkling of an eye the rapture is reserved now exclusively for the church. With the rapture of the church, the Lord himself will descend from Heaven at the trump of God and we will be raptured vertically from the Earth to meet him in the air.

It's the fulfillment of the Lord's prayer in John 17:24:

"Father, I will that they also, whom thou hast given me, be with me where I am; that they may behold my glory, which thou hast given me: for thou lovedst me before the foundation of the world."

This kind of body, subject to sin cannot enter into the eternal state. A translation or change must be necessary before we can enter the kingdom of God. Therefore, there is a change at the rapture and the body will become incorruptible. The mortal living will put on immortality through translation.

TWO END-TIME SIGNS

Apostasy

"Let no man deceive you by any means for that day will not come unless the falling away comes first and the man of sin is revealed the son of perdition." Thessalonians 2:3

The apostle Paul warned of this spiritual departure in Acts 20:28 and Timothy states;

"But the spirit explicitly says that in latter times some will fall away from the faith paying attention to deceitful spirits and doctrines of demons."

This falling away comes first with deception enticing people out of the spirit into the flesh for self-gratification, self-promotion, and gain.

"But take held to yourselves lest your hearts be weighted down with carousing, drunkenness, and cares of this life and that day come on you unexpectedly." Luke 21:34

Revealing The Man of Sin

"For the mystery of lawlessness is already at work, only he who now restrains will do so until he is taken out of the way." 2 Thessalonians 2:7

The manifestation of the sovereign authority of God is evident in the restraining of the lawlessness. The presence of God's people here due to the holy spirit dwelling within and working through them helps prevent the mystery of iniquity. Once the restraining influences are removed nothing hinders or stays corruption. We will behold the utter powerlessness of man to walk in the path of righteousness when the divine grace is removed. We believe the restrainer is the omnipotent Holy Spirit who indwells all born against Christians. Thus, all spirit-filled Christians will be removed before the antichrist comes to power. When the Holy Spirit is removed as the restrainer, the antichrist will take his place in the house of God – (The temple) and the Apostate church. Wickedness cannot co-exist with the Holy Spirit which stands in direct opposition of the spirit of lawlessness.

TWO MYSTERIES

The Mystery of Iniquity

"For the mystery of iniquity doth already work only he who now letteth will let, until he be taken out the way." 2 Thessalonians 2:7

The rebellion of Lucifer against the authority of God initiated this iniquity characterized by its lawlessness and independence of God. Working through the anti-Christ with lying signs and wonders Satan will manifest himself in the flesh. This hidden power of lawlessness is present in the world today but will increase in the end times with the man of sin coming on the world stage. As Christ was the son of God then the anti-Christ must be the son of perdition. He is called the mystery of lawlessness. As our Lord was the son of man and the son of God in one person, the anti-Christ must be the man of sin and the son of perdition. He is the fruit or the result of lawlessness because inequity is the opposite of godliness.

The Mystery of Godliness

"And without controversy great is the mystery of Godliness, God was manifest in the flesh, justified in the spirit, seen of angels, preached unto the gentiles, believed on to the world, received up into glory." 1 Timothy 3:16

God was manifest in the flesh being born of the Virgin Mary by the Holy ghost, thus Jesus came forth on earth being the son of God. Revealed in human form and vindicated by the spirit our kingsman redeemer was God's saving grace to a fallen world. God's revelation of his redemptive plan in Christ was hid since the foundation of the world and is the heart of our Christian faith. This Godliness of God's son is now to be reflected in us. So the mystery of godliness is Christ living through the believer.

TWO TRIBULATIONS

Tribulation

"In this world ye shall have tribulation, but be of good cheer, for I have overcome the world." John 16:33

The concept of tribulation implies persecution, affliction, pressure, and suffering. We will pass through trials and troubles such are called birth pains and the beginning of sorrows.

"We must through much tribulation enter into the kingdom of God." Acts 14:22

Christians cannot come under God's wrath but are required to endure tribulation for a season on Earth. We need to be steadfast and immovable in the midst of a perverse and crooked generation and an ever-increasing tribulating world, picking up our cross which includes suffering, rejections, and persecutions.

"And not only so, but we glory in tribulations also knowing that tribulation worketh patience." Romans 5:3

Great Tribulation

"For then shall be great tribulation, such as was not since the beginning of the world to this time, no, nor ever shall be." Matthew 24:21

The great tribulation is a specific time frame in revelation. God's greater severity of judgments and wrath leading up to the second coming of Christ. The great tribulation is the end of the dispensation of the age of grace and is characterized by an atheistic religion headed up by a world ruler who magnifies himself above God. The remnant of Israel will be brought to repentance through the sufferings they will endure under the judgment of God and the persecution of Satan. Great catastrophes occur as seals are broken, trumpets are blown and vials are poured. The great tribulation sees the antichrist rise to power, the false prophet, the erection of the image of the beast, the wheat and tares harvest, the fall of mystery Babylon, the battle of Armageddon, and the return of Jesus. The great tribulation is a prelude to the second coming of Christ, making it clear how necessary divine intervention in the world is both for judgement of the wicked and deliverance of the saints.

TWO CHURCHES

"Be thou faithful unto death and I will give thee a crown of life." Revelation 2:10

In Revelations, we see there are Two praiseworthy churches, Philadelphia and Smyrna. Philadelphia is a perfect church of brotherly love, keeping God's word, and not denying his name. They have Missionary zeal, great love, and tremendous works.

Smyrna is a faultless church that thrives through adversity and persecution. They were physically poor but spiritually rich.

PHILADELPHIA - Perfect Works and Brotherly Love

Philadelphia kept the word of the Lord and didn't deny his name. Restoring the original position of the church, they rejected all traditions, creeds and opinions relying only on the authority of the Lord. Their love for their brethren, fellowship, charity, evangelistic, and missionary movements doubtlessly earned them a promise of being kept from the great tribulation. Called the perfect church they refused to compromise, continually teaching the truth and doing God's work. With their love for Jesus and faithfulness to God this vibrant productive church achieved some influence feeding and nourishing many. Although persecuted their missionary zeal sought and taught the truth and kept the patience of Christ himself.

SMYRNA - Physical Poverty and Spiritual Wealth

For Smyrna, Jesus says no matter what tribulation they face he is there with them and reminds them he is the first fruits of the grave giving them strength to overcome everything befalling them. Remaining faithful until death will relieve them of their suffering and earn them a crown of life. Like Myrrh, their suffering produced a sweet-smelling fragrance to God. They faithfully performed in the name of Jesus bringing the word of God in the face of opposition and persecution. They realized their citizenship and treasure was in Heaven not here on earth.

TWO WITNESSES

"And I will give power unto my Two witnesses and they shall prophesy a thousand Two hundred and threescore days clothed in sackcloth." Revelation 11:3

My Two witnesses implies that witnessing is their business. As the Two witnesses who stand before the God of the whole Earth, one will bear witness to God as king decreeing his commandments, while the other bears' witnesses to his high priestly ministry. These Two foretell of Jesus' reign and prepare the world for it. They relentlessly proclaim the gospel while remaining humble but powerful. One bears witness to God's righteous rule of law, while the other bears witness to his mercy and grace. They provide testimony on the things they have seen and know. These Two anointed ones are associated with the laying of the foundation of the house of God, These Two candlesticks and olive trees are pointing to God's agenda and purpose. As to their identity Moses and Elijah, both stood with Jesus on the mount of transfiguration. Moses turned water to blood and was the only body the devil contended over. Elijah is quoted as saying as the Lord God of Israel before whom I stand, called fire down from heaven, withheld the rain and is said to come before the Lord's return.

"Behold, I will send you Elijah the prophet before the great and terrible day of the Lord." Malachi 4:5

The Two sons of thunder, disciples of Jesus, asked if they could call fire down from Heaven, and if they could sit on either side of him in Heaven. As pillars of the church, could these be the Two witnesses? Only Two men are recorded in the Bible as not having died, Enoch and Elijah. They both had a ministry of judgment and they were also the only ones who have ever been raptured. The identity of these Two still remains veiled but may become clear in the future.

TWO SPIRITS

Spirit of Truth

"Every spirit that confesseth that Jesus Christ is come in the flesh is of God. Hereby know we the spirit of truth and the spirit of error." 1 John 4:6

When we receive Jesus, we receive the Holy Spirit. This spirit overcomes for us and makes us alive to God sealing and stamping us with his image.

Spirit of Error

"For many deceivers are gone forth into the world even they confess not that Jesus Christ comets in the flesh." 2 John 7

The spirit of error confuses, divides, separates, and destroys God's truth. The spirit of error works closely with the mystery of iniquity to prepare people for the Anti-Christ. The spirit of the Anti-Christ is the spirit of error and leads people into error because the world cannot receive the truth because the whole world lies in the power of the wicked one. This anti-Christ spirit always works through the zeitgeist of the age such as it is now. This spirit gets you to believe and trust in this life and this world. It leads you away and causes you to depart from sound doctrine. Without a love for the truth people are willfully blind and led astray to believe deceptions. Drunk on seduction and deceived people seek after a sign and only a wicked and adulterous generation seeks a sign. To sum it up the spirit of error comes from the anti-Christ in the spirit of the age with false Christology and false prophets.

TWO KINGDOMS

The Kingdom of God

"For the kingdom of God is righteousness, peace, and joy in the Holy Spirit." Romans 14:17

The kingdom of God is a realm that is under the authority and sovereignty of God.

After being translated into the kingdom, we stand up bearing witness to the gospel manifesting God's will. The kingdom of God is already present in the ministry of Jesus, but its fullness will only happen when Jesus comes back. We must recognize the value of this kingdom, for this spiritual kingdom accompanied Jesus in his first coming.

The Kingdom of Heaven

"And I will give unto thee the keys of the kingdom of Heaven." Matthew 16:19

This relates to the eternal purpose of God in relation to his kingdom program, the right to rule, the realm of rule, and the exercise of royal authority.

The kingdom of heaven is the sphere of righteousness, the realm in which God rules a kingdom with the manifestation of his authority.

TWO NAMES

King of Kings and Lord of Lords

These Two titles express absolute sovereignty over all things. He is also our King and our Redeemer. The Alpha and Omega, the first and the last, proclaiming he was at the beginning of creation and he is at the end. He is the author and finisher, judge, and ruler. Lord and Savior, faithful and true, wonderful counselor and good shepherd.

TWO-EDGED SWORD

"Out of his mouth went a sharp Two-edged sword." Revelations 1:16

This sword has many functions, one of which is to separate the soul from the spirit. After the fall of man, the spirit was so oppressed by the soul that it knit together. This then requires the word of God to separate it so we may live fully in Christ and not from the soul anymore.

"For the word of God is quick, and powerful and sharper than any Two-edged sword piercing even to the dividing asunder of a soul and spirit and is a discerner of the thoughts and intentions of the heart." Hebrews 4:12

Thus the swords dividing happens when God's light shines through his word exposing the self that was previously hidden. Only the word of God reveals the way to liberty in Christ. Truth itself is Two-fold and hence the word of God is likened to a Two-edge sword. First a revelation and second our responsibility to it. The path of truth is like that of the Just, it shineth more and more.

After Thought

"How long will you halt between Two opinions? if the Lord be God follow him: but if Baal, then follow him." 1 Kings 18:21

To those who never followed Jesus, He issued a calling, to those who wanted to follow him, He said pick up the cross, to those who volunteered, He said to count the cost and to those who hesitated, He said to let the dead bury the dead.

Bibliography

Major Bible Themes – Lewis Sperry Chafer – 1926
The Sheeriyth Imperative – Dr. Michael Lake – 2016
Corrupting the Image 1 & 3 – Douglas Hamp – 2011
Changed Into His Likeness – Watchman Nee – 1967
The Falling Away – Dr. Andy Woods – 2018
Unveiling Mysteries of the Last Days – David Hamblin – 2010
The End Times in Chronological Order – Ron Rhodes – 2012
Faith Alone – Arnold Fruchtenbaum – 2014
Sinai to Zion – Joel Richardson – 2020
Things to Come – Dwight Pentecost – 1958
Come Lord Jesus – Watchman Nee – 1976
Ancient Epistle of Barnabas – Ken Johnson – 2010
Biblical Mathematics – Helen Vallowe – 2014
Giants, Fallen Angels & The Return of Nephilin – Dr. Dennis Linsey – 2015
Shadows of the Beast – Jacob Prasch – 2021
The Sovereignty of God – AW Pink 2nd Edition
The Rapture – Ken Johnston – 2009

Thy Kingdom Come – D W Night Pentecost – 1990
Things that Differ – CR Stam – 1996
You Can Hear The Voice of God – Steve Sampson – 2015
The Messiah – Todd D Bennett – 2010
The Final Words of Jesus – Jacob Prasch – 2005
Ancient Order of Melchizedek – Ken Johnston – 2020
The Lost Prophecies of Qumran – Josh Peck – 2020
The Great Mystery of the Rapture – Arno Froese – 1999
Reclaiming the Rapture – Douglas Hamp – 2017
No Balm In Gilead – Jacob Prasch – 2022
Gleanings in Genesis – Author W. Pink – 2011
Israel & the Church – Amir Jsafati – 2021
Bible Quotations – KJV
Numbers in Scripture – Ein Bullinger – 2020
The Final Nephilim – Ryan Pitterson – 2021
Footsteps of the Messiah – Arnold Fruchtenbaum – 2014

About the Author

Timothy Patton currently resides in Southport, NC and has been a student of Bible eschatology for the past 20 years. This is his first book, and he is already looking forward to the second book, Counterfeiting the Sovereignty of God.